KAY ULANDAY BARRETT

WHEN THE CHANT COMES

D1126843

TOPSIDE
HELIOTROPE

Library of Congress Cataloging-in-Publication Data is available.

ISBN -- 978-1-62729-015-9

10 9 8 7 6 5 4 3 2 1

CONTENTS

kamataryan: death · · · 69

kapwa: soul · · · 87

For my ancestors, my auntie yoly, my lolo guillermo, & my mama.
Look we made it!

For every sick, disabled, brown, queer, boi, chunky, poor, outcast.
Every single one.

WHEN THE
CHANT COMES

katarungan justice

if your family is forced here

1.
You will have to manage cities and scraps on the same tongue.
Whole continents are rapture and fantasy
as your languages, every one of them, turn their backs on you.

2.
To crave dirt on land that you cannot even touch.
On the best of days, miles are suspended in disbelief,
you fester on smells that can't be placed
but have home in your bones nonetheless.

3.
You can text message fast from years of phone card dialing
in panic. Because you miss the ocean. Because your lola
fell once again. Because money.

4.
You watch people march on TV in a city that is vague
or your mama's misbehavior 20 years ago.

5.
Something about
hindrance.
repair.
authenticity.

6.
Just because you eat the food doesn't make it yours.
Just because you eat the food makes it all that you've got.

7.
Anywhere you enter renders a heartbeat as sharp as a catheter.
You wait for signs of home, wait in small drips,
pangs into your blood that are always too hungry.
About your blood, it's always everything and never all at once.

Rhythm Is A Dancer

Growing up, I do remember "THE ROYAL"
(pronounced like the first names "Roy" & "Al,"
for usual big gay pyrotechnics)

thursday nights as young
queers teemed in logan square
armed with body lust that could
squeeze out teenage awkward
in just one dance.

Being in 1998, under 21, for $5
we could outwit our muscles,
discover them,
boys with eyeshadow glitz to match their
graf on avenue walls,

the pants or shirt you were forbidden
to wear at home
(due to whatever that check box
said on your birth certificate).
Our mamas probably would have
slit their wallets
if they only knew where
their work hours went.

We kissed hard.
                    We held hands.

Spoke our mother tongues
Cheek to cheek, with our "bestfriends"
who were really our girlfriends,
even though being 16

meant a new best friend
oh every 6 months.

Managed "it's time for the peculator,"
in the veins way before hipster
upswing tattered property taxes,
disemboweled heart
of brown queers everywhere.

Way before white and straight folks
took our moves, bought
our clothes or put holes
in their own to call "vintage"

Some like Joanna aka Johnny,
depending if you were her father
or his lover, banished shadows with cig butts by 3am
and gave this glare like he knew
exactly how to hold you
if you needed it enough.

Or Celía who could out
pop AND lock ANY b-boy
and move her hips stunning to freestyle
swerving more than kicked snare drums.
The following morning,
girls would itch the lines of
their palms for those
angles.

Or the kids that assembled rum
And sugary juices
to forget whatever
they were or weren't coming home to.

or the bois
who laid down their guns
at the door for a long
slow dance.

or them,
that one queer who had The Cure
and Depeche Mode buttons all over their jean jacket.
too cool in the corner
who shook her legs a bit
particularly in appreciation of
salt-n-pepa, and maybe it was
a trick of the strobe lights
        but she even smirked a little.

Or us who rounded out
summer stars & sky with soprano notes.

How glorious could we have been
lodged in lockers by school day,
scared of the lies that mirrors told?

We came home breathless
from dancing our queer bodies
back to valid,
each time we'd make
a ruckus
as queer as brown
        not to reinforce stereotypes,
            but to take back the
                space that is ours.

The space in our ribcages
and in Chicago's sidewalks

that would coax us
to love.

We come from ancestors who drum and dance,
who made sweat rivulets alongside the tears
because movement had to start first on the the body,
before the noose,
before the well-intended missionaries,
before the semi-automatic rifles
before the rich studied our rhythms,
before the empty and angry,
before the straight and the narrow
beat us,

We found beats.

Now when I ask you,
  Giiiirrllll? What was the last jam you danced to?
  I mean reeaaallly danced to?
Sometimes I wanna hear your song,
Sometimes I'll wanna listen to your beat,

But mostly
I want us to celebrate,
to honor,
to love,
all our movements.

For Andre Leneal Gardner,
Edith Bucio, Prerna Sampat

Survivor's Guilt

in the winter, cardboard boxes hold bodies he
cannot forget. four walls, a dog, heating, stove.
cardboard boxes are slain over his eyelids,
eyes open or closed.

remedies used to be a nickel turnt to a trick to
a stranger you wouldn't have to say hello to again
but the sweat of them still stuck.

he carries those hippy granola bars everywhere now.
he's become that social worker you hate.
not exactly like the white ones, but maybe worse, because
he was one of you. he let's food hang out with a wallet,
with dogeared books, and letters he's never going to send.

a scarf is wrapped snakelike on a scowl when the first snowflake
hits sidewalk. *where's the bathroom? where's that dollar?*
how about you put on plastic bags over your feet then socks?
no problem man, I understand rough economy, maybe
some change next time?

his cough is the timbre of skeletons that didn't make the cut.
1 outta ten. 1 outta ten make it into a home.
he's that special snowflake. the back turner.
to pretend normal, he thinks a furniture set on sale
and a good painting are meant to be easily attainable
like a hot meal, doorknobs that can lock behind you.

today a nightmare placed his cheek on the sidewalk.
a jawline pushed to iron down a thirsty dandelion.
black shoes and batons beat at his spine.

one drag queen, two trans women, and one butch
are ushered by the cops.

he wonders about christmas. christmas decorations.
how torn ligaments are ribbons can keep the skin at bay.
seasons greetings.
greet things.
grieving.

and he wakes up naked,
not believing the rent he pays is any kind of remedy.

Uncertain

Uncertain, I come to crying, just crying.
Soluble tears, imprinted on the lines on
notebook pages and my lover's cotton sleeve.

The weight this body
holds includes my mother's voice, her clock
runs by overtime shifts and the current warring of her
birthplace can't enter her mind,
she doesn't have the time.

Besides, she's sent the manila envelopes
with withered money, she's sent the boxes of used
shoes and brand named clothing for family back home.

*

Who was it that said
in AMERIIKAHHHHH you are RIIICCCCHHHH
   (rich rich rich SO rich)!

Whoever made such a lie, hasn't felt helpless
underneath his own skin-
body limited to manual labor and factory blue-collar
hours spitting out your happiness,
   (in spite of the poet or thinker parts of you)
day in,
         day out.

Whoever made such a lie never felt the burden
underneath their skin, to be the brown illusion
to white-eyes in an all white academy.

*

There are egg rolls on the table, next to the
dominoes pizza, paces away from the coca cola
chilled in the fridge. The perils of my culture--
decoratively spread before me upon my welcome.
we sit and listen, our heads down,
my friends all beaming activists, all
theorists who consider a night
deconstructing any documentary
as fun filled.

No academic institution had the
words my mother had,
the veins
in her arms
permeating blue cross HMO insurance
that barely paid for half a prescription.

her hands roughened
from cooking, her eyes glowing like
the laugh of a child. She spoke commonplace of
her captivity:

I know two places--
work and home
work and home
work and home.

A needle-sharp pain is in her breathing;
her accent sways our names
as I look over to
the face that will be mine in thirty or so years.

*

I've seen my mother precarious at 10 years old,
jumping rope with the neighborhood kids and me
our mouths sucking the juice from paleta sticks,
our bodies ragged from sucking out the summer in a day.

We couldn't extend ourselves to
believe the sweat and sacrifice of
our parents then.

Now, if we're lucky we study them--
have harsh nightmares
about the secret screech of our parents,
of our elders, that will soon be your own.

Cry out in gutted sentences
cupping hope knowing
that it isn't enough to
be a woman or poor or immigrant or
a person of color or queer, but
enough to fight against being fragments.

*

The u.s. finds it fit to send in 2000, 3000, 5000
troops this fall and trample on a constitution,
                              I've only read about.

It's charted land like my mother,
tasting her freedom,
even after it never arrives.

*

Yesterday,
I held my mother close,
and of the three languages we know,
our skin is the softest.

She wrapped up fried foods, their scent
in our clothes, on the cracks of our mouths.
"sorry for my little house,"
the same voice that pounded into my ears
that report cards were methods of survival,
said this to my friends.

I sit here in my room now
plagued by those words,
waiting for the ending of a poem that
that refuses to apologize.

Never The Forest

Does it really matter what city I am in? Tacoma, Montreal, or Ewing, I can step into a hotel room after hours of being en route and a smell, a specific odor triggers me. Once it was an elevator that I swore smelled like the sparring ring, sweat highlighted with the rounded knobs of toes, feet in clockwise routes, spit. I smelled the exhausted breath circulating through calcium deposits, the cough of bruises yet to show to the eye. Instantly, I could feel the sting in my shins, my fists go to a clamped defense, teeth-gritted, my neck ready for wind-shift as simple as a leaf in october subconsciously avoiding a puddle. Body memory is beyond muscle.

This time however, in hotel room 203 I stepped into him. His arm hairs with curved backs, the slighted nicotine at every syllable and waiting breath. I remember being age 12 and my mom spitting up the words, trying to avoid eye contact, "He tied you... tied you at the ankles." With what, I thought? A baby lynching, I kept thinking only later, much later did I look at horrific images of small brown and black children tied up for war, for the new land conquered, for the land stolen from under the feet of people who had lived there and thrived there years before. Academic institutions try to brace you for the effect with free pizza, but those descriptions never leave you entirely. My story isn't this story. It was the small po-dunk Michigan gilded with dirt roads as much as frogs and cattails and bales of hay. It was this man, my half-brother, who was close to half my mother's age, haunting me, who made her look down at the ground. Not the store clerk who shifted her eyes at the suspiciousness of our presumed brown sticky fingers, not the bank teller who spoke excruciatingly slow to heathens she obviously couldn't help because anything else was more important than proper customer service at that moment. Not even my own father who loved her, this white nature photographer, who took her away into this smaller than small town, left her to the snow and a trailer park home and microwave dinners, made her pupils focus just so on the floor.

We couldn't look at one another in the eye. "Do you see those scars on your ankles?" I looked at them fondly, rubbing them like my own private jewelry, a string of slices over the bone, now lighter than the rest of my skin. I glanced like a child would at a secret hiding spot, only I knew the secret password to. He had tied me at the feet with fishing line string. I was an ad-hoc science fair project of his mind. He did this when I was an infant, couldn't have been older than 3 years old. Must've been three. This is what I was told, anyway. What are you supposed to remember at the age of a toddler? I have no recollection of this, of me being trussed like a spring chicken for a family dinner. I assumed the scars were like my birthmarks, or my indented dimple, just always there at my first breath. According to my mom, I was wrong. Her face was practical when she told me, almost medical - she told me these things in the daytime. I remember looking out through the window at the trees, yellow finches bathing in the birdbath, one finch dissecting its food, a poor wriggling worm. I exhaled and looked at the bird. It prodded with the singular focus as much as any surgeon. Any words being said by an adult or child vanished.

He did more afterwards. His name was Forrest– as in woods, as in trees and nature and animals tumbling along the great countryside. Those were all my favorite things. Living in the city as an adult, I always referred to myself as Midwestern, as someone akin to nature, saying proudly that I used to live near the woods, never the forest, no not that word. Never that word out loud. The woods, I would insist.

Right off the highway up to the north of the lower peninsula, up michigan mitten's middle finger, he pumps gas for a living, is missing a few teeth. Slim Jims are a reliable lunch break, just as they were when he caught toads as a boy. As a teenager, I would watch my mom ignore him, not ever leave the room when we all shared the house. Her feet, bricks. Saw her ask him to leave or kindly see his way out. Saw the veins in her hand bulge as she held onto the doorknob, locked all the doors and doubled checked them in her head, linger a little longer on the final bolt, longer than she would for any other visitor.

Fucking hotel rooms, man. I'm in a hotel room with patchwork carpet, Room 203 smelled like this. Smelled musty and mud-laden. Smelled like fungus making bed on a good sturdy tree or like the mold accumulated on wood holding the foundation of a house. Ewing, New Jersey couldn't have been farther away. As I stepped into the hotel room, I pleaded with the modern lines of furniture and bright colors to erase the country smell of him, to bring me to the present, to 2010, not to the late 80s of shag carpeting making waves between my fingers. I noticed the window. As I opened the curtains I saw trees peppered by red hot and orange blistering maple leaves. Bright and pronounced, I allowed the colors to warm me. I opened the windows as far as they could go, I caught a distant glimpse of a flock of birds who readied their wings, full bellied from a morning meal. Some shook in the flurry of the rain. With the fall breeze on my face, I pushed the metal angles of the window hinges until they made an honest squeak of boundaries, as though to say that's enough now, that's enough.

Brown Out Shouts

this is for Matea who dances the bomba
with hands that crest moonhips
and who admittedly, kisses harder than she loves herself.
every trans, genderqueer, futchie, fairy, AG, butch queen,
anything with roots arches toward her, their arms like petals
soaking up her light.

and this is for hard ass Krys who doesn't want anything
to do with brasso or that jrotc uniform, but just
wants 3 meals a day for his brother
and a brand new binder for his chest.

for Javi, who takes his tequila quick.

for Aqua Starr Black.
because they had the bravery to re-name
themselves: aqua. starr. black.
sometimes you just gotta call out your power
cuz no one else is gonna do it for you.

Maria is a dancer clasping onto hardwood by the heels
but serves our coffee at the diner always wit' a smile
and always with her hair on-point.
she's pissed off cuz her partner cannot afford to go to the hospital.
although, you can't see it, her heart breaks because no papers
or government can explain how this person in the bed
makes her laugh like a guttural fool.

for JP who draws sketches sneaking them in your purse.

for Celiany whose caliber demands that the very least of her lovers
have the following traits:
dexterity, initiative, and someone who can "lay it down."

for every son shaped in bullets, your heart as compact as
a trigger, your voice a sharp wind song that wants to lay a forehead
down on the chest of your boyfriend.
let your letters survive the wars, jail cells,
let the meter of your words swoon your lover back to the bed,
as you take turns turning off the alarm on the nightstand with
your toes, elbows, orgasms, and in between kisses.

for that lonely Korean guy Jake who found me in a group of
500 white people in the frenzy of the Sugar Club in Dublin, Ireland.
I make do he said.
We've got one grocery store and I practically live there.
I mean, my kimchi is decent.
we can still see him shrugging
in the strobe lights, hungry for somewhere else.

this is for you this afternoon, spring cleaning your blues away,
maybe in your favorite t-shirt, maybe you called in sick,
maybe your body rattles, maybe missing your pamilya back home,
maybe you are waiting for that next shot to find home in yourself,
maybe your voice is hoarse from asking strangers for food,
maybe you lost a loved one or are about to lose yourself,
lost in the whimsy of musical notes,
the rhythms can consume the sadness, if you let it.

for my dearest Sarwat who sat on a hill, held up the sun,
looking at all the fiiiine transgender and queers of color
and said without saying,
Umm. I am not going that plenary/workshop/speech. You go on ahead.
I'm gonna stay here. mm hmmm, I deserve this.

for español, pangasinan, patois, pidgeon, mandarin
love poems you write.

for those babydykes and trans youth who sprout out from
the neighborhoods described to tourists as,
don't go there. its dangerous.
rolling up their windows from our existence.

for you who fights for our rights,
for you who laughs too loud,
for you who eats too much,
for you who twists wrists by paintbrush,
for you who will not let your spirit pass up a sunset or a protest
even when you think you deserve less sometimes.

for you
because there's a brown out right now
and by that I mean there is no electricity,
which means life is crashing and pouring down

and by that I mean I am lonely,
which really means
that we are brown and trans and queer and out
and we've been told too many times that all of those
cannot belong all at once. that based on those odds,
we equal death.

for you / for us / for we
because without explanation, we exist
and you, you like all of our ancestors before,
you live it so fiercely that even when injustice sets in,

this rumbling sky houses your breath and
that is better than any survival story,
that, that is joy being born.

mahal love

Psalm For The Mama Who Turned 60

For she who sang to young ears old country time radio and
   malinak lay labi

Bring forth the father who is now a cloud roaming.
Bring forth the mother who was a severe beating and only before
   she died,
an apology accepted.
Bring every sister back in her likeness.
Bring more than eleven at the table, passing steamed pots and
   she the oldest
reminding them   *be careful now.*

When I visit her in the basement we watch Filipino news,
corruption   murder   bribery,   she shouts.
your voice pitch planted next to Malacañang Palace,
gripped to the throat of anyone who steals.

Ask the auditor, second that motion / we both were born political.
Make her vice-president of another organization:
Mangaldan, United Pangasinan, Rizal Center.

Bring cables that travel to Quezon City microphones
of Sharon Cuneta and Aga Muhlach
—I'm against nothing that makes her laugh and sing in the bed.

The permanent marker is in the top drawer,
         write down large letters S A N F A B I A N
         onto a cardboard box. A cousin gets her old tape deck radio;
         she carefully includes white tube socks, hats, our smell.

Let toe step be center of the dance floor, her cha cha cha, her
boogie—

knees bent like busy elevators, both men AND women in line,
her child used to stay up late /
do you know the time? they'd whine.
of course she knew the time, she worked the graveyard shift
    since 1990,
        three more songs, anak. just give me three more songs.

Look carbon copy / my face, eyelids, thick hair to her louder left
    dimple.

For the mother who told the daughter to be architect of her own city:
    No one will build your dreams for you.

Bring the games of poker and pusoy;
claim some hearts and diamonds somehow.
strategize. collect. make the best possible combination.

Nanay, when you are tired,
when the last cigarette has flickered,
Akong bahala sa yo.
Relax na, let me take your turn.

Midwestern Queer Love For Brown People

she knew these tenements, studied my chest
and memorized how i like to be kissed.
fists were hour long measurements
pronounced by scratch marks.

but
she didn't know how i liked my rice.
but
she couldn't say my name.

didn't think of philippines, of skin color,
of why i was tired of explaining what "privilege" was,
of anything but what her own hands could do.
her actions taught me white people can't really
get it unless they are
the hero

this poem is not written in the prospect of
saving anyone, but it's the same regret until I learn
   something new.

in this life, flower petals are dried in your favorite books and
leave stains that blur a sentence you've underlined.

sometimes it is the singed wicks of a good smelling
candle, a spark of a child's cherry bomb—
that starts the worst of fires.

in this life it takes
too many times
to actually mouth the word
"enough."

someone can remember the cleft beneath
your ear and kiss it as gentle as any petal,
but this doesn't make ever make it right.
someone can revel on the beach but pollute its shore.
none of this is basic need.

we can do without the kissing.
none of this could possibly say:
cry it out, you're alright,
cry it out, you're alright.

Letter To My Unborn

if I were stronger, I would've
had you like I planned—
alone in a hospital bed, legs thrumming,
out of breath, as your new instruments
figure their ways of being.

guarantee: we would be as necessary & vague as hungry homeland
dreams, the both of us as far as an atlas is to any newcomer
in this nation. we would wander, drift, resemble the lost
balikbayan and worn luggage, we would send messages
in passive aggression—
        an uneaten bowlful here, a haircut
        born from rebellion there, we would keep secret
        blemishes from one another, just like my mother and I.

why the tears on your pillow? your parents not normal enough, huh?
slinging organic foods & social justice pages! (so embarrassing)
we'd be the lark of your college campus, our perky smiles
as you hid behind a tree or a finals exam.

republican amerikkka would scowl at you,
stampede its haunches on your spine.
I would just wince at your banana
                    republic sweater set.

(couldn't you just spit dead prez, beatbox in your daydreams,
unicorns-goddess-forbid you were to ever break
the back of a guitar string to upset your neighbors?
your cousins are social justice organizers & cultural workers
striving for liberation...! How you are my child?!#@)

tonight I bled after 3 months, some miracle, my lover sleeping
never knowing by nightfall I ache for you to lay between us.
maybe, if it were up to lips or foreheads or strap-ons,
when we can plan you by the minute,
we would never let your breath arc from accident.
—-if you came.

do not think I haven't stated your case. could you be born of
auntie idna's kidneys? of my taste for cholesterol or her too easy
opts of silence? what about your own hoarding resolutions--

I promise: this is the last cigarette, last kiss, no seen bruises
   next week.

and your other parent? she writes down long lists
to never imagine you. her own life steeped in survival
assigned before she could crawl or cry.
for her, your skin isn't thick enough for the wars,
the television commercials, the artist's income or hunger.

gratitude for living is not enough.
if she were to anger a hand your way,
   she would be her own mother.
      you would only be the proof of something they have in
      common.

never knowing you were, she adjoins hips at my torso
as I crest lullabies and whisk the ceiling cracks
to a diagram of your limbs.

my dearest anak, I swear
even the bedsheets make mountains
where your belly would be.

not all moms deserve cards

I.

not all moms deserve cards.

not all mothers protect or
hold their children as
delicate
        as
                they deserve.

sometimes
moms are bribes,
        bludgeoning,
                with tongues that chase you
whenever you get a chance passed a mirror.

they can be bruises you see around your arms
(so carefully not in plain view).

my mama was the strongest point of the backbone
whenever we collided:
a shock, a fracture, a jolt
you cannot express   in even your homeland tongue.

2.
it's complex, we know this.
colonization tells brown mamas
to be the android and the shell of themselves.

the graveyard shift & the serving white people
fuck up a person's sense of time, of self.

these reasons you relay
   when your hair is too short & you weren't invited to places,
   when she asks you for more money,
   when you realize there are no photos of you together
   since you started using "he."

it's what makes the violence different.
it's what makes her death poignant.

missing thousands of miles is the unbearable
whiplash & the pact of mothers with their children.
there's no refund for this type of awareness.

3.
when other people have brunches
sharing their new boos in awkward introduction,
with mamas that move them in & pack their favorite foods

when a mom chirps proudly, uses the correct pronouns,
is there at the doctor's office, can pay for your new car
or lets you stay at home to save money,
or whose resemblance doesn't feel like a storm
where there's no shelter from, understand that that's not
     everyone's world.

it's a privilege.
family privilege.

not everyone can "work it out with time."
when someone knows you when you were
fumbling and friendless at age 9,

sometimes you even become your mama,
dream up the possibilities of what never was,

you long for
someone
anyone
          who lived
          stayed
          bothered
long
enough at all.

I want to call and ask you to come over

you'd say, *of course I'll be there.*
   the story ends with your exhale at
   the nape of my neck, our palms an eclipse.
   our legs in the manner of tree branches and quiet.

that's all I want with you.
the need and the leisure of our blended breath.

   just the thick delicate shape of us after midnight.
   that's not what is happening. instead, you and I are beyond miles.
   we are rivers and roadways apart. if I think too hard about it,
   I even start to hate the wind between us.
   We're so far, we might as well be strangers.

don't try to console me with,
   well, at least we're under the same moon.

at least the moon gets to see you beam in person.

I wish I was the moon.
if I were the moon maybe
I'd understand the rise and fall, the variation of us.

if I were the moon
   maybe I wouldn't be so worried to
   shift my own shape just to get the chance of you.

When An Earth Sign Loves An Air Sign

She is a Gemini.
Have you ever tried onto the wind?
                            It doesn't happen.
She's the kind of woman
who doesn't wait for you
to watch your couple's TV
shows together, because well,
                        you don't really have TV shows together.

The better question to ask would be:
Are you even a couple?

But you fuck anyway,
fuck hard, fuck into all the I love yous,
until only gusts capsize from your mouths.

You ride into one another
like oblivion or like the day depends on it.
She buys you your favorite sandwich, doesn't
glare the way your ex still glares in your nightmares,
remembers her own worth,
so you figure, this poem could end better,
           this poem could be beautiful, you think.

On a text message from the desert,
           she sends you a photo of a sandstorm or tornado,
           some combination of the unnameable.

You picture her hand stuck in a frame
as the earth twirls, as fragments of desert and
wind lash up to an incomprehensible sky.

She'll remark from afar.
    She will not drive directly into the heart of it,
    you can count on that.

You wonder if she gets it—
This love that you both experience.

You won't be able to explain
that you feel dizzy after you kiss her.
The moment is glorious to watch and witness,
sure, but what will be left afterwards?

Nightgown

I.

The night before the "chat" I wrapped my face
with your green nightgown, the color of the turtle painting
you delivered by way of midtown protest, Harlem, now in my
   living room.
yeah, the nightgown, the one you kept in the middle drawer.
I knew this would be my last time with your smell.

I inhaled whatever parts you left by accident.
I managed to review any lesson I may have missed.
The way you rolled over with a leg stalled over mine,
the scrawled nail marks on the wall.
I think I made that up all along.
I end up doubting my own skin.

2.

Previously:
See our juice like graf all over
my sheets? You're everywhere, baby:

       That's not graf. Those are marks made in
       hieroglyphics, those are the marks we made before
       time, waiting for us to get right here,

                        you said

smirking.

3.
Inhaling you, I mumbled: *Let my body memory be a compass.*

I didn't say: *I love you.*

I knew you wouldn't accept this fact in person.
(only maybe in a daydream that I don't dare entertain anymore)

Right now, I cannot look at any lips without yours being the signature.
Right now, my walls keep their inquiries quiet as I cry smelling me,
which basically is smelling you.

This is proof that yet again
that skin beats cloth,
wishes beat reality,
every time.

To Be The Prayer Nobody Told Us About
For Sonia

There is sanctuary
in the way we practice our old ghosts,

    when we can make them something bigger than
    the monsters we fiction from fear.

I don't believe we are the warnings the
rosary beads warn us to be.

Look, I made it alongside with you,
                still breathing.

We wrap our legs something biblical,
                still breathing.

We christen palms guilded by eastcoast winter,
                still breathing

Where saints and titas don't give us closed
minded stares on the rush hour train
or the quick walk
on the bad hip of a weeknight.

We still come home to our wet warm harvest.
There are no exit wounds and we are not stolen.

We bear blood before the ash. Yes, rejoice:
There's a name for people like us.

You joke that you're a *good catholic girl*
And I wonder what "good" actually means for folks
like us.

Because there isn't enough scripture for our stories
and I have to confess, I was never any good at prayer.

However if I get to fall asleep to her exhale,
I can recite the science of her bones until the heavens

believe us real,
believe us so.

Homebois Don't Write Enough

homebois we don't write enough love poems.
we re-name ourselves izzie from ~~Isabella~~,
casey from ~~Cassandra~~, kay from ~~Kathleen~~.

we run out of ink for our stories cuz we've been
running through doors of male and female, never satisfied.

we stunnin' baggy jeans and bright colors over the sirens,
we stop cars and walk with stride that makes the concrete
self-conscious about its own stability.

at the tip-toes of summer,
there you go talkin' about how you
                "need a femme pregnant and barefoot."

as I shutter asking,
                are you gonna find a stiletto ready to stab you
                if the night sticks don't come get you first?

asking- are you gonna be that bullet that is a mouth?
asking- are you gonna be that missile that blasts your woman
  until she misses you,
                even when you will both be in the same bed?

if we make ourselves harder than bone,
make us a legacy that is beyond all this.

cuz I've been running through doors of male and female,
never satisfied.

that makes you nervous doesn't it?
are you worried, your palms sweaty

because I am *NOT* that kind of a man
AG
stud
butch
boi
warrior
partner
son
brother

and that might make you obsolete, that means this whole system
needs a revision. that means, we have to ask ourselves daily
                are you are doing your homework?

homebois, we don't write enough love poems to ourselves.
spell out our soft syllables unapologetically, letting
our strength beyond stiff jaw and cold silence,
the stuff of abandoned buildings.

let us unfold the photos with us dipped in lace and dresses and
     laugh and maybe even   keep it, rejoice!
let the most tender cipher surround us not be our mother's tears
     for the loss
               of a daughter.
let us hold our breaths for the Sakia Gunns and the Fong Lee's, as it
               could easily be our sweat on this sidewalk.
let us adore the swiftness of kisses in moonlight rather than the
               pummeling cusses of strangers scared of difference.
let the tensile ace bandage be a testament across this chest,
     waving like prophets of a gender war. ,

let every poor black brown and yellow mixed race queer see their
     way into
a paintbrush, a camera, an uprock, a computer, and not into the
     hips of
hand grenades chucked on someone else's homeland.

to every person who squirms in the bathrooms, classrooms,
and on stages next to me:

let them know that this moment is a clue of your queerness.
let them know my titas are at casinos burning this American
    dream away too
let them know my kuyas christen their kid's foreheads and give
    me daps
with the same hands.
let them know that each time they make fun of us,
they could be in a feather boa, singing Prince, showing
their loved ones force that will push them toward and not away.

let their children run up and down the city
as the confident trans queer kids, who get scholarships to college
    & sustenance
for a GSA or for promoting safety at school, for writing poems in
    their sickbed,
(& you being the backward parent they divulge to teachers they
    are ashamed of).

let me not reveal my monster each time I hear
        "I'll fuck you straight."

let my fingers not be readied trigger, grabbing sharp objects
for stabbing back.

let me walk away
        without harm, disbanding my razor-edge that could
        cut their lifelines, slice steel song into their temples, shear off
        their pride as soon as they start to unzip their pants or call the
        cops.

let us know we can do this and make it clear:
we choose not to.

let us know we can do this and make it clear:
we choose not to.

homebois,
if we can make ourselves harder than bone,
if we can make ourselves harder than stone,
    make us a legacy that is beyond all this.

On Longing The Fantastical

My secret dreams Craigslist ad goes:

"brown amerikan mixed-race tender queer tibo
(former teenage beauty queen) at heart transman
seeks kindred yet platonic times w/ someone similar.
if you have stances on palabok recipes or the emo
nature yet sexism of pinoy rock music, appreciate
the patterns of bow ties and banigs, please give me
a shout. if you are known to sulk at your own reflection,
or are you never enough for yourself, and/or too much
for others? come, let's talk about it. if you long for razor
sharp wit without the lacerations on the spirit, let's hold
hands. priority will be given to those who don't want
any political bullshit, who are for justice without the
righteousness. would love someone who has a thing or
two to say about contemporary pilipinx/pin@y cuisine via
diasporic interpretation or mixed race manhood. rigid
gender assumptions and amerikan vegetarians who
won't dabble in lechon once in a blue moon, will not
be contacted."

karamdaman sickness

Connection Flight To Santa Barbara

The airlines wheelchair assistance worker calls my name.
Tito Jun squints and looks for me, not knowing I'm what he's
    gonna get.
He says, "Are you Pilipino?" then hums indistinctly,
    something guttural
yet nonchalant, then smiles weaving into the foot traffic.
                You see, that's how Pin@y people do.

He tells the presumably Latino gentleman whistling
as he looks at my passport to "be good," whereby the
    friendly man says,
"I'll try but only till noon."

They both do a jiggly dance,
some moves that shift both their comb overs,
a juncture that could happen often, and Tito chuckles,
"This one – he can dance!"

It's 8am.

They exchange sweet smiles,
a pat on the back longer than three seconds,
longer than a cough.

For checkout, I go to pick up my own bags,
he holds a gesture for "no, no I got this," his arms veined and
    layered,
swollen like an impending stormy cloudy sky.

We both find ourselves stuck,
both stammering for pride.
He, with his age maybe and I, with my body likely.

As I go through checkpoint,
he watches me closely,
guarded, too cordial to the next TSA agent.

We get through faster than usual,
no gender checks or pat downs.

I plop into my wheelchair and as we near the gate he
    mumbles,
"Check point can be too stressful for some people, ha? Not fair."
I squirm into the chair.

I give him an extra good tip, a "salamat po"
to his gentle "walang ano man! ingat ha?"
and that's the first Tagalog I hear in the morning.

He waves super big and goofy,
strolls off as he begins to hum away.
It sounds in tune whatever it is,
like something faint but something whimsical,
something that'll keep you smiling
whatever your destination might be.

Crip Sick Tankas: A Performance Series

conjure
Did our families
ache for freedom? Did they clutch
wishes to their God
to gift us windswept choices?
Bless their stress. Bless us for trying.

questions
when he winces she
asks "is it the pain or is
it the heartache?" to which the
reply usually is:
both. together they just sigh.

sdq love
pause. let's stay true to this:
use your imagination.
our love is a cryp-
tic new dance, a new rhythm,
i crave your fumble inside me.

what you have in common
offer me your mouth
like a sunrise, a willed stretch
spread unstoppable.
tell me about your loud curves:
ask me to wake up for you.

gender confusion
doctor says "are you
wearing shorts?" but they are my
boxer briefs. "oh," he
squirms, until he avoids my
gaze. I chuckle secretly.

dogkid #1
you're better than the
codeine bottle in palm's reach.
save me always, guy.
I love you too, soft pillow
eyes, whiskers, snout. ah, slobber!

dogkid #2
pops, does your body
smell like a thousand shrieks
by trains or lost things?
I'll rest my jowls here, okay?
I'll breathe where it hurts, okay?

ex-partnership
To have our dogs get
along & drink coffee the
same way is like win-
ning the queer lottery. Still,
it made no difference.

breakfast sometimes
Take a spoonful of
three day old leftovers like
mashed potatoes or
takeout rice whichever is
the best vessel for pain meds.

breakfast again
at 1pm when
you've scraped all there is of your
fridge, fuck yourself but
do not think of your exes
or their soft hands.

netflix
Netflix will vacil-
late between your nemesis
& savior. Let it
be. Dark rom coms with a
quirky female lead, will save.

when your body outgrows your friends
*where you at? you're in
bed on a Tuesday afternoon?
well, what happened to
you? not all of us get to
have vacations. yeah, must be nice.*

it's hurts bad, so now is a good time
our feet are on fire,
we wish anxiety didn't
mean this. I wish you would admit
you were sick. though, I let you
take me in, twitch fist, top you switch.

check-up
the nurse fumbles my
chart, she calls my stuff "junk" now
as per my request.
this change makes us both smirk
and who says safety ain't real?

switch
I don't say top.
I say *however we*
land, how's your hips? back?
This bed is sometimes all we
got. Throb it out, in, around me.

daddy
when two royal queers
in pain arch backs, it's like a
swinging of planets,
collision, princessa,
just name how; be good & ready.

fire
Begin to let the
refrain take us both down.
my earth sign likes the
deliberate. Will we melt?
If we're honest, I hope so.

Folyamory #1
If Secondary
Bill of Rights is my bible,
then you would be an
atheist who left it up
to fate fumbling the sacred.

Folyamory #2
I used a religious
metaphor because I knew
you'd hate that. Okay, hate is
a strong word, but if it's any
-thing like abandon, we're cursed.

pre-op
when they call you to
surgery, they call you by
your assigned at birth
name. you laugh and hand them a
cup full of pee. fair trade.

Requests That Come From The Rain

I.
i'm writing because of the rain.
my body shaped to the songs of landslides
and even with a heating pad, i'm in need.
body like stiff.
body like clay.
do you understand this architecture?

the grimace you make is beyond a prescription note
or one-time only Get Well! card.
what you don't tell them is how you can crumple
and pour without warning or watch,

how in pain you wake, tremor, laugh,
how you pause, grasp, buck and brace,
as you move move move with
            and rebel it,
                        this pain.

whether, it's the knock of a rib cage
or a highway of nerves in bumper to bumper traffic,
        no childhood scraped knee can prepare you for this.

before the rain falls,
your joints are somber sirens.
people may see it on your face or not, it doesn't matter.

it doesnt take long to learn, some storms rumble before they
    land on skin.
it doesn't take long to learn, that it doesn't matter if others listen.

maybe you can't go up the stairs today.
maybe even your own bed is too far a trek.
lesson: the breath is both a lullaby and a scavenger.
how to uncoil is near ecstacy.

where does the loneliness go?   here.
where does the inhale steep out to a cry?   now.

what?   I didn't volunteer for this gift.
                It's just how I happen to be.

2.
when your breath makes no treaty.
drool on the pillow, toe slick stumble unsteady,
fog fate to stammer slurred sentence.

ancestors know our groan like kept beads,
clung trees to the root, steaming pots of the oldest fires.
our people, we know too much too often what it's like to burn.
circuitry of   skin, muscle, spleen
in the sheets? the kind that makes you
        a hermit while everyone is a parade,
        while everyone is laughing at the party,
                as nerves rip raw.

3.

baby, breathe.
baby, crumple like the smallest pebble
or pour like a giving sea.
baby, wobble into me.
you are a cliff of both a cackle and a wince.
your nerves unfurl to the most daring place to be.

I am writing because of the rain,
my body shaped to the songs of landslides,
and even with a heating pad, aspirin, turmeric, tintures,
        i am in need.

body like stiff.
body like clay.
i am sure you know this architecture.

4.
i'm likely in love with this viciousness.
somewhere in me has to cling to the surge
because that's often all i've got.
the pain always shows up and when the people never do.
i've had to do this to stay alive.
                        still. remind me would you?

baby, breathe.
baby, crumple into the smallest pebble
or pour like a giving sea.
baby, wobble into me.
you are a cliff of both a cackle and a wince.
baby, your nerves unfurl to the most daring place to be.

If it's hum or howl—
if those are our only options:
then please, will you just rock with me?

*For SDQ POC Facebook group, Fatima Arain, Setareh Mohhamadi,
Aemilius Ramirez, Kiyaan Abdani, Mel G. Campbell, Leah Lakshmi
Piepzsna Samarinsinha, Ejeris Dixon, Manish Vaidya, Ki'tay Davidson,
Aurora Levins Morales, Billie Rain, Sofia Webster, Bekah Fly, Taueret
Davis.*

YOU are SO Brave.

& those scars i had hidden wit smiles & good
fuckin
lay open
& i dont know i dont know any more tricks
i am really colored & really sad sometimes & you hurt me
—ntozake shange

What happened? Aw, sweetie, here, let me get that for you. What do you mean "No thank you," You don't want my help? Some people are ungrateful,   I was helping YOU. You are SO brave! *Please step on the scale, Please step on the scale, Please step off the scale.* You are SO brave! I've never seen someone one on a dance floor/ protest move like that! What a pimp!   Can I touch your cane?   *Does it hurt?*   **"People with disabilities are often seen as "flawed" beings whose hope of normalcy rests in becoming more like non-disabled people or on becoming "cured." —Sins Invalid.** (When will you get better?)   Don't worry everything will be normal soon. If you just try hard enough, you will heal. If you just pray hard enough you will heal. (Have you tried acupuncture? water therapy? meditation?)   If you take these herbs enough, you can be like you were -   better, normal. Why   are   you   walking   so   slow? This is the city of the hustle, son. Buck up. If you can't speed up, leave. **Dear _____; I understand that you have accessibility needs and we as a queer progressive organization** love (love love love mmmlove) **your work but we unfortunately, we find your requests to be unrealistic. We understand that you are a queer   and   transgender   and   p e r s o n   o f color   and   with limited income,   but we cannot fund you at this time.** *Please do send us samples of your work so that we may distribute them to our participants   FOR FREEEEEEEEEE!* *Dear [insert assigned-at-birth name you no longer identify with that*

makes you want to cut yourself at every syllable]; It has come to
our attention that you are 100% disabled. You cannot work at all.
Disabled people don't work at all. They should never work. Don't even
consider working.   (Does it hurt still?)
*Classification: No prolonged standing, walking, steel pin impacted
osteoctomy aiken mcbride. Constant deviance in the foot based
on affected use. Constant deviance. Constant deviance. Constant
deviance. Cane usage to support impediment and prolonged
limp.*   Oh   my!   Look.... at that hair!   Don't
you   have   a boyfriend to come to physical therapy with you?
**"Seen as 'flawed' beings whose hope of normalcy rests in
becoming more like non-disabled people or by becoming 'cured.'"**
*For the report we're going to need to see some ID, [insert loud guffaw
here] that cannot possibly be you. you were attractive once! What
happened? Please step on the scale.*   So, you were attacked?
Whatdidyoudotomotivatetheattack?   What exactly does L G B T Q
mean? Well, Ma'am, we have to use the biological sex it says on
paperwork. It'd be nice if you wore some lipstick, maybe some
make up? It might make this whole process easier.
Does it hurt still?   Hasn't it been years now? Why aren't
you better? Based on your old life, don't you want to be more like
me?   Heeeeeeey! Do you have a fundraiser? **I don't
know any disabled people personally**, but we can raise funds to
help YOU, because we think YOU deserve it. This is the city of the
hustle, son. Buck up.
        YOU. DON'T. KNOW WHAT YOU ARE DOING!
Give me that, you don't know how to take care of
yourself!   **Ugh, you are so slow. It's hard to
imagine you could do anything yourself at all.**
You are so pathetic!   (Does it hurt? Still?)
Yo homey, we're all going to the club! Should be some cuties there.
Oh, yeah.... yeah, there are stairs dude. Oh yeah, sorry dude, I
forgot.   *The march is 2.5 miles long, maybe you can meet us
at the rally?*   Aw, look it that little boy with the cane! Why
do I have to get up?!#^@   **You want my seat faggot?!**

So... (long exhales) you were attacked? Why do I have to get up, chink?   Hey! I'm talking to you! Do you uh-speak uh-tha-engrrriish?   **He doesn't even look disabled.**   If you have any concerns around safety at this event/conference/protest, you should really bring up these concerns with this cisgender rad skinny able-bodied person who confuses wellness work for **everybody gets better work!**   Wait (laughs) is that supposed to be a girl?   Awwww, you look so cute when you dance! Let me take a picture of you holding your back - *show the cane! SHOWWW THE CAAANE!*   What did you do for someone to attack you? You must've done something to provoke it. Please step off the scale. You know if you lose weight, you'd be healed right?   **We'll help you because we think you deserve it,** (not like some people with disabilities), the ones who drool and make a fuss.   *Constant deviance.*

Constance deviance.   *Constant deviance.*

(You'll be normal soon, won't you? Won't you?)   It's not far, just a few blocks. Aw, I know you're in pain, but you can make it, dude.   What do you mean "No thank you?"

you don't want my help?!   *Please step on the scale,*

Please step on the scale,   *Please step off the scale.*

the sky makes promises

There's an aunty with brown eyes,
as rotund as her hips
near the garden.
As the clothes wisp in the breeze,
she considers
          maybe pepper or ampalaya?
The sour tart like cusses when you tell
somebody too much truth.

She does this arithmetic,
feeds her family dragon breath,
slices tender potatoes,

every bite a forgiveness
every gulp a spell to ease the empire sting,
every swallow an anointment to shield
them from this awful country.

1992:
Feed them flame.
Warm bellies to house flicker—

they'll make it
(she mumbles)

they'll make it.
(her bones creak a chorus).

On the corner of Albany & Waveland,
clothes on the line blow in the breeze.
The sleeves dance among the clouds.

Fastforward 2004:
from a hospital bed,
a sunset adorns her flesh by dusk.

She reminds me,
> *The sky makes us promises, apo.*
> *You have to keep them.*

Dedicated to Dark Sciences People of Color
Dream Retreat 2015

to be underwater & holy

every survivor is splendor.
every spoon is sacred.
every cough is an altar on the bend of ribcage.
every cane is a drum calling into the earth.

you will be told that you are not worthy of a party.
you will be told you are not a celebration.

why exist at all?
because breath is an exhausted ship lapping the wind.
because your muscles are the fatigue of a sunset.

when your bodies are carnal waves collapsing,
remember: together we can find the shore.
together we can rock and wave and rest and float, together.
we need to move together.
together we can rupture veins into storms and
together we can be the grit as promising as the sound of shells.

our lineage tells us
there will always be land and ocean
in our bones.

after every shift of tide,
no matter the catastrophy,
please hold on if you can.

here's a promise:
dare to press an ear against my chest
and on this love,

we'll grow scales for every current,
we'll part every sea like scripture.

For Brianne Moore, LeShaun Lovell,
Geleni Fontaine, Kit Yan & Ro Garrido

kamatayan death

Somewhere A French Braid Is Intimidated

I know you are looking at the tower of it, the bouffant of your grandma's past is pacing and Marge Simpson has written long-winded letters. James Dean applauds me as he looks on at the mortals. This hair, peaks like a perfect whipped cream signature, looping a hook, like the faux-hawk you wish you had. All finesse.

One could wrongfully mistake it as another limb, but not as clumsy. Clutching tree branches, reaching over the cobwebs of the top shelf, dislodging your bag of chips from the claws of the vending machine. Every part of my body has purpose. A burly man at the pizzeria on 14th st. knows how he survived with the dashing assistance of my jet black Heimlich maneuver – as gentle as a mouse, as smooth as any scalpel.

Once, I dreamt my hair was at the helm of a steamship heading east. When I woke, my fingers were cut by beach glass and wood splinters. Nowadays, brushes get snapped in half, my favorite hats burn in a pyre unprovoked, plus the migraines. You can only spend so much money on pomade. You can only spend so much money on pain killers.

I was told when my first cowlick sprouted that my great great great tita Crespina blessed me with this gift. She was a healer and welder after all, who needed no help as her tendrils had the utility of a whip and a diligence with the mortar and pestle. According to legend, she took a swift slice to a trespasser who mistook her butt for public access. They reported a bundle of split-ends french-braided to his esophagus prettier than a bow-tied ribbon on christmas morn; his mouth eternally shaped to ahhh.

There is your warning, I wouldn't make any funny moves. Just a suggestion. Even I keep watch, but my eyelashes hold hands to keep me from the wrath. I wonder, are they are as frightened as I am?

Kuya Bong aka "Stealth"

everyone called him Bong,
  with a captial B.
      he was the scrawniest of the crew, cap backwards, lanky
        mothafucker.
      His uprock was the brown sears tower,
      that solid.

there was a pause under his hightop step,
  a pause when he entered a room.
      pare, they would call him, *brother*, they would call him.

quietly looking into the night sky
the young men exhaled smoke rings,
drifting air into the stars.

                    he did this with them,
                sidestepping the crass talk.
          he always made a new space,
      a new shape,
a new opening for himself

        even if you didn't see him right away,
           even if you thought he might vanish.

Nibaliw Beach, 2007

It doesn't matter how many times you read
Philippine Society and Revolution,
your amerikanjeans   amerikanwalk   amerikantalk

are never enough to raise your
mother up from a Dagupan City Hospital
bed.

Poem won't will air to her lungs,
doesn't raise enough money in
time for the ticket to see her last breath.

No article or placard can pluck the IV
from her arm, the bruises like wilted
stars. One for every amerikan dream,

or every cigarette break, or every
tear riding on the wind of phone cards.
You child, are only a teacher,

only poet at best. You curve Tagalog
on paper or by mouth just enough
to supplement copies of a death certificate.

You can work a college classroom enough to name your
   pains.

Honestly? You are only a translator calculating years by
   balikbayan boxes.
On the mantle in Pangasinan, you are forever

a size O, forever waiting for a husband.
You are the name you were born with
by way of your white father's best intentions.

You will glare obsessively at statistics by
megabyte, afraid to admit you look
exactly like the dead.

You will come to realize there is no option
to hold your mother's hand. It will be in her
ocean as your arm curves to corals,

where you will imagine the waves resting
as she calls your name.

in bedstuy when you've lost your lola, your mirror

on the first day the world is without her, you are stuck in bedstuy. stranger's arms are swathed around you like cocoon and storm clouds and other things that are beautiful but uncomfortably scary. *it's not right. people shouldn't have to go back to the homeland just because of death.* older women and queer warriors held me. we in neck deep in sorrow even though the wind still came, the skies were still blue, children still jumped in sprinklers, petals still perked on their stems. i hated and admired the earth for her reliability. *breathe, look in my eyes,* i wondered if these are the lines that they had to receive when their last elder died. i wondered about how inheritances aren't about lawyers & money signs.

my auntie, my great aunt, she's the new dead on her way to gabriela silang, bob marley, sylvia rivera, and depending on the day, my mother, has become a hero of all the forgettable.

i.
a sweeper of the back porch you forgot
existed. the creak made the roaches
unfold their arms.
she needed cleanliness only
the way some of us must read books.

ii.
a bringer of warm canton to tito boy, his lacerated voice all san miguel and the same love song he sang when he landed in this country, the same chorus to women he can't remember. slurping his noodles, she lets him stay another month, again. ignoring the warnings of him being a free loader, she knows what it's like to stay misled by the dream that this, *this is only temporary, this badly*

dealt hand, this unreasonable lover, this lost job, this crude country.
maybe this is how we are all related, the drunk uncle, the giving
auntie, me. unmoving with our love songs on repeat.

iii.
a seeker, her eyelids like streetlamps.
when you were kicked out, she had it out to find you,
to nestle compliments close to your skin,
to at least keep you warm into starry unforgiving chicago.
the same woman would cloak you when other women
in your family cursed your lack of skirt-wearing and
your manly carriage. she called you anak, said
your mom will stop hitting you, i'm sorry,
all the while she kept a close eye on the altar of
steamed bangus fish and rice placed for the ancestors.
this she knew would help them seal the deal of my safety.

iv.
a blender. as early as 5am, she would blend food to a mush for
her toothless bastos husband. after 40 years he called her *bruja!*
as everyday as picking his nose, scratching his balls, his unclean
hygiene for picking out the worst of traits. she took avocados, corn,
bananas, feeding this man of ungrateful curses, making her love
as easy to process as possible, watering it down daily.

v.
a slow mover as she aged.
my mom would steamroll past her,
smoke on her heels, a scoff soon to follow.

auntie just chuckled as though to know
each step is a blessing, whatever the pace.

i would be arm-in-arm alongside her,
let the hotheaded speed forward!

we'd be as far as a block behind sometimes and not care.
the both of us unintentionally intentional
felt the earth hold us steady,
felt our gaits stretch like generations of patience.

i love your company, baby. thanks for waiting.
i'd smile as her secret nephew, *akong bahala, auntie!*
our one-two, one-two, shuffled a resolve
that can still be heard all over the northside of chicago.

For Yolanda Ulanday Salvo with the support of
Sharon Bridgforth & Omi Osun Joni L. Jones

read this whenever you are tempted

The sound of arms and legs are never the answer
no matter how wide they open.
Remember this the next time.

When the bedroom curtains draw like elephant skin, so heavy.
When the bed is the jigsaw puzzle and you are the only piece left
or willing, let yourself plan the next breath and the next
in play by play, improvise.

The sheer act of an exhale is treason.

Don't wanna wake up even when your body says yes?
It's alright to say   *I can't do this.*
Let it be your handwriting if it must.

Let your tongue be a failed suture, a switch, a brick,
the flint before forest fades to the ground.
If you know the pit, the bottom base of burning,
you know where a sprout might have wriggled.

It's okay to not trust anyone,
deem that every hello has some ruin on its skin,
spit out that all you want is to lay down,
just wanna
lay down right   *here.*

When all the sky you have in you
is a bird's wing cleft
tumbled to a highway roadside

be easy on yourself,
you aren't the first or the last.

For you *ideation* is beyond an idea
when you text, "10 , I'm at a 10" is not a drill,
when you are all stakes,
no poker face,
only room for the give up
and the give in,
all limbs and skin are the white flag in full mast.

Take the razor of your pupils to the curious
and pay no heed, as your heart is no different.
All hearts palpitate when they notice
the subway trains come round,
think "one step further"
close their eyes to hope for the best
of heartbeats to come
back into their breasts.

or pray for the taste of rust to hit the gums.

You will be a high tide of
No   no   no
when hymns of flesh or tenderness row your way
let you be the last drop of whiskey beyond the flask.

Allow the haunt, bring on the ghosts of ghosts that brought you
here, sometimes we never learn until our own spirits have no
    howl left.

Embrace the course hands of a stranger,
let the crass and the need be all you can give.

Leave the party early or stay
until your tears are the only
tinsel that remain in the room.

It's okay to lock up every opening,
reinforce the hatches and hinges:
journals, doors, ears, mouth.

The last prayer or poem,
that is your call.

Appreciate when the feel of static is your inhale,
when all the hours press up on you as you are
coated in citywide pulses,

Oh, hollow husk of a heart,
don't let the beatings of regret
be your only song.

Everything Down At Your Feet

We do not count names on a wall for memorial
or pan our pupils to stacked missing persons reports
or cuss the cops dismissal of another body fallen
in the ghetto.

We do not pray the rosary walking from
station to station, eating only the foods
that remind us of the dead, accepting howled
sounds for voices of ancestors.

We aren't catholic or don't make the sign of
the cross at every cemetery we drive past.

But we do feel guilty.

Finding passage to our next midterm
paper paragraph, day job, reluctant dentist appointment,
we were jaunted into closed eyes,

this Monday.
we wanted
to put
everything down
at your
feet.

It's not the shrewd news of it,
of the procession of death
from phone call to phone call.
War makes far worse.
But *you*
you made us who

haven't spoken or look each other in the eye,
call long distance for your message.
"There was no note."

Your face
couldn't have said the word *cliff*,

we didn't see the hurt you drew around yourself,
the lines near your eyes we assumed were from
squinting, not from this.
How many questions do we have?

How come, was it your father's fists?
Did you unlike so many of us, take notice of north
america and look away?
Did you decide no matter how temporary,
that the world was too much?
Did another passer-by call you faggot mincing
another good day?
Was it a trigger, like the way
we have nightmares in lover's arms
or did you make the decision and
only got so far that
gravity came to answer?

That moment or never.
Jump or stay.
Jump or show us letters of the boy you
kissed whose laugh reminded you of the harpsichord.
Jump or talk about the intrusive phonetics of English.
Jump or send us emails of you in your
latest brunette wig & heels hailing a just mopped dance floor.
Jump or have a tendency to tell your crushes too much
right away.

We working hour after hour in
attempts to
re-build your smile back memory
so when we look at photos
the thought of only two-dimensions
is a vile insult.

There are obituaries written in three languages
constructed with tears from countries
I never you loved.

If you were
to just
come pick me up this Friday night,
you'd kiss my cheek in silence
your best feather boa wisping as gallant as a cloud,
ready with your fist
held up to lips like a microphone,
a Madonna song would burst from speakers
and only you could coax the refrain
out from my mouth.

Ways The Philippines Can Talk

Being amerikan,
you draw in a journal about escape plans, arcing a fiction
of getaways —here you cannot ease your way into a café,
or walk to a bus station without being stared down,

ma'am? they'll say glimpsing to the haircut, then cutting pupils
towards the breasts.

American feminist queer theory has no grip as you buy gum at a
    store
near the sleeping goats, or hold breath next to the baskets
in a northern province. Ocean salt finds its way into your
    everything.
Karabaos don't give a shit about your gender pronouns.
Your family scissor words as your name skitters to the floor—
Tomboy,   I hear,   *fat, dark, like a man.*

Titas shift the kanin on their plates as though they
could trim your fat, extend the length of your hair,
sprout a loudmouthed husband at your side,
all with the slightest bent joint.

Then they turn to your beloved, exercise syllables
like she's supposed to parade in them
So tall, so thin, your skin so light like a model—you can't be Filipina,
Koreana ka ba?

The comparisons are said the same as any harmless observation.
Convictions of divide and conquer are tossed like habits.

There doesn't have to be a white man to make these claims—
our own people learn how to harm enough,
choose the right words, translate to English without flinch.

You both can hold hands b/c   this is what <u>friends</u> do.

After midnight you assemble your limbs back to
their rightful place as you rid the pressure formed
by all day heat and no privacy.

Poverty is two small bedrooms shared by everyone at anytime
and you hate that you want to go home,
for free wi-fi, ache for your bed.

Mostly, you hate the fantasies of sand & revolutionaries
right before the plane left the ground.

i might be ready for heaven

The plane saw me as unwanted cargo, much like this
country. The stewardess gaped at my fat arms, bulbous veins,

her maw open like she's never seen a brown woman in pain,
even though we are everywhere.

Your seat,   *your seat,*
she pointed.

You cannot put me away.
        I cannot be contained. Not anymore.

As I left, I had the gumption to close the car door, my daughter
had a face like a talisman, eyes shimmer a sacrilege, they follow
    me everywhere,

        You cannot go with me, next time, I said.

She will see Nibaliw beach as the bangus smoke wafts in her
    hair, but for now,
it has to be this way.   These are not my last words.

The car door pressed up against her palm. I did not want to see
what her
face would do at an airplane gate, I did not want us to
remember
each other this way.

I would take ~~her~~ him with me, I would, but then I would have
    to tell
the truth and he would have to tell me he's not my daughter

and even though I might be ready for heaven,
I am not ready to be told I've been lied to all these years.
        America did enough of that bullshit.

My organs are chockful of collapse, my kid has done enough
    already.
They'll find out soon, we never had the same home,

whether I kicked them out or not. I never belonged here
with my childhood of typhoons,
our bloodline wasn't a promise we'd survive.

They'll find out my body is a high tide that finally took over the
    shore.

I just want to taste the salt sand from my childhood again.
I've waited too long.

Take me there.

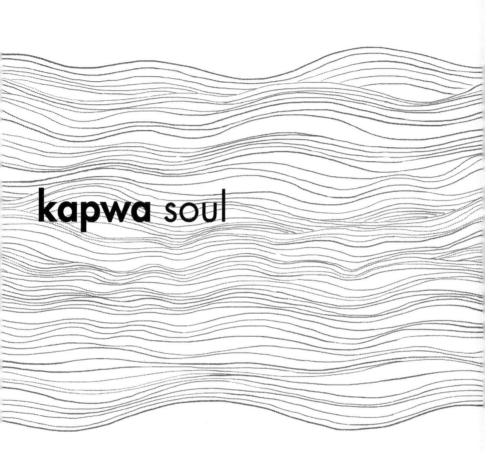

kapwa soul

When The Chant Comes
in gratitude for Andre Leneal Gardner

i told him what she said.
how i told her about getting top
surgery and being ready to be on T,
how my partner's immediate response was,
    do you want to be on T or get top surgery because
    you think you are fat and need to lose weight?

        how this broke me.
        it broke me.

he sucked his teeth.
a trustworthy mannerism we both got from our dead mamas.

he and I go back the way queer hungry parched kids can go
    way back.
back to alcoholic boyfriends
        wearing bandanas and girlfriends who
        couldn't keep their shit or dental dams together.
            he remembered back when we were small
            and queer and always dancing and didn't give a fuck.
            we clocked in makeouts before cellphones scheduled
            them for you.

brown kids ate chips from 7-11 in logan square
with deep deep house music still on their hands.
our northside and southside pride had only the pact with the
streetlamp sauntering when the club closed.

    i hated my chest then.
    always have.

we are no longer that young or that bold.
he's now in LA waiting tables, singing ballads like he did when
  we met.
he attends daily meditation sits.
he's had years of me waging this hate for my body.
my long distance news made us hold our breaths,
hold a moment of silence over phone wires.
i told him there has to be a chant for
this. he said,
baby, i'll breathe, meditate, love you,
and tell you
        when the chant comes

Pogi, Guapo, Cub

bois grown up from fisherman towns,
farmer towns, riverbed towns,
all mama's bois,

bois working to get through college,
bois with stains on their hands from
late shifts and immigrant sensibilities.

 bois called *pogi*, called *guapo*, called *cub*.

the first trans men I saw were in salsa bars,
all of us in starched collared shirts, our hair
carefully constructed with pomade,

I watched them swing their partners,
as they danced a
dervish of skilled figure eights.

Together
 we're
 horn,
 drums,
 decadence.

the balance of cowboy hats and their shuffle
of manhood made the strobe lights

 swoon flicker thick.

the chest, the jaw, the needle,
make no matter with

drunken balls
of the feet.

to brandish brilliance
means to be made from scratch.

Alberto V05

Before I knew that banners were electric and
stonewall was a riot started by Black & Brown women who
could've been your friends,

You were my babysitter, long blonde and red hair,
wigs along the wall of your room.

1990:
Every morning over frosted flakes I'd watch you.
By sunrise, a mascara brush coughed truth on eyelashes,
clouds of Revlon rouge lifted your cheeks,
it became obvious
— to make ritual took fuss and finesse.

My first up-do, first sequins dress were by your hands.
I learned to admire femme fierce babaylan
as you could watch soap operas and poise
a cigarette on the edge of the mouth while updating
hair highlights on clucking aunties.

You listened to which husband was a *sonofabitch*,
which child was on the way to Fs.
You had neither of those to complain about,
but they dropped their lives into your hands, an unjust
equilibrium.
In turn, your perms were something infamous.

Everyone trusted you, tita
with their nails, their gossip, their biggest affairs.

When you shampooed my hair,
the label of the bottle read ALBERTO V05.

I bragged,
> *Is that YOU, Tita?!! You've got YOUR own brand!*

you shrugged,
> *Not yet, baby. But soon...*

Kids don't always know that compliments can be too honest.

United Philippine Calendar Girls Show, Hyatt O'Hare Hotel:
I had an obscene crush on Sheila Rodriguez.
You knew it and let us hold hands as you fixed my face.
I hated wearing dresses.
> *My, how husky you look in those high heels!* said everyone.

Not you though, you told me it took work, coached
> *This may not be you, anak.*
> *But you will shine.*

You were responsible for my make up at every pageant,
and I wonder what it took
for you to take the tomboy out of me?

How you saw a child in and out of
petticoats who gazed with longing
at the escorts' crisp tuxedos.

How the elders made you in charge
of their looks under the bright lights yet
never invited you with them to the stage.

My talent that evening ended up to be martial arts.
I broke boards with lipstick on flying over toddler butts,
and to your creation, my makeup didn't
smudge at the sweat.

My bow after was for you.
You let me be myself

and so I hugged you tighter than any rule
ever imposed on our bodies.

If someone asked who did my makeup,
I boasted, *My Tita Alby!*
She's the BEST beauty queen I know.

There were no lies here.
We looked better
than we could imagine
only because
you made it so.

For my tita alby

sparring self

for every tube to the vein,
anak, where are you?

each poem,
each hour she works into another wrinkle,
a trace of a cancer spreading,
                    punch,
her bad cholesterol anyway,
                    kick,

the worry, the worry,
poetry doesn't pay enough,
punch,

she says she feels too lonely, debt,
as your college student group screams
bureaucrata-capitalismo! ig bagsak!

                    punch, punch, kick, punch,
miss.
                    punch. punch. punch.

my lola/her mother, not enough money to back home,
    not the right
papers that fold, just their spirits folded onto a
    photo in the pocket
of the pants they wore when they got into this country.

not. enough. link card, link card, welfare case,
calling card from our first coins.

a lecture: phd professor said jokingly
   if you make less than $20,000 in this country
   ya might as well be holding a styrofoam cup,

send money home, empty,
   Kick!
no milk & honey, in this country
they lied....
   Kick.

each line, her hands like mine, brown ache,
brown poor, why she smokes cigarettes
until holes burn the inside of her liver, poems are
fraud and a sorry excuse for a daughter,

         miss miss miss, kick!

the sorrow on her eyelids as
the collectors turn away, quiet,

an opened bag of chips hidden,
         punch,

they say "if you've got heart disease, then you probably
have high-blood pressure, diabetes,"

         kick,
stop,
         punch,

not enough money
not enough money

once we played word association game
as she waited in the doctor's office it ended with

the words,

       crying
       and
       too much,

    punch.
       kick.
       ki – punch – ick,
miss

dear lolo; i know that she prays to you
       punch
calls to you in her dreams, you brush her
cheeks with your thumbs, she admits
       punch
she wants to go somewhere she thinks
is heaven & you tell her to wait
       punch
       punch
the cries run up the
pipes and vents at night
and she can't work anymore,
and she can't work anymore

she can't,
    punch
move.
    punch
not,
    kick.
enough,
    punch
kick,

          // poems.

mixed race in mackinaw city #1

his body hummed by radiator and snow dashing against sill. the
tea kettle hasn't wailed yet. no steam spattering into the calm air.

the slush is building up he thinks. he cracks his knuckles. car tires
spew stuff to the sides.

block other parked car doors, their owners anticipate the chill seep
into their shoe linings before they even leave destination. grumpy
commuters wishing they had pulled blankets over their heads at
first sight of the window, wishing to have the luxury of stopped
time and indoor heated activity. secretly, he never hopes for snow
shovels or an armada of diligent trucks on-call with their faces
masked with shoveled snouts. he wants landing. he wants it to
stick. he wants snowsuits and yarn wet mittens to drape over the
heater vents just like he grew up.

you'd think him a motorcycle guy and easily mistake him for the
avid bicycle lover that he has always been; fuel conscious, speeding
feet, night wind singing over eardrums. maybe a scooter gay with
a soul patch and black clothes, a brown jamie oliver-type zoom
zooming from farmer's market to haphazard kitchen cooking for
a nerd book club in any major city of the u.s. empire. he chuckles
at this never happenstance, thinking of himself all eco-privileged
and skilled.

the first spiral of land, first wrist-jerk dodge of an obstacle by control
of handlebars were by none of these. he was a rural kid first, mind
you. on his dad's side, his white merchant marine father's side,
were builders of the mackinaw bridge, hard construction hats on
oiled faces and years later he would clap his palm on the bridge's
iron elbows, be right under the grates and could see cars driving
overhead on a still and frozen day. the only way he could get there

is by snowmobile. the cast of spray from tall hills, he sat in front, the wide glass glistening blues and yellows on horizon, speed and snowflakes just pouncing velcro winter coats, two scarves on and goggles.

he knew that his life was direct contrast to the summer before where his mama talked about fishing nets, no air conditioning, climbing trees scraped by fresh durian and buko, t-shirts and shorts for everyday attire, fans and tsinelas for needed accessories.

Dream Lineage

i. **Lola / grandma:**
Cowry cackle
your body will create warnings
  she tells her oldest born.

Soft girl married to a poor man who
throws rice in bowls, ties globes of rice grain
  to t-shirts. Made her grandkids walk about with said globes of
  congealed   dreams   on their hips.

Hold onto the achuete, keep crystals close, neighbors on Albany St.
  have sorrow in their hearts,
  paychecks missing, sick children coughs,
  they beckon for you.

  Make the coconut oil. Go to the santo niño, the black one, and
  hum hail marys,   hilot,   massage.
  Tell your secrets, the forlorn & fragile.
      All your cries at night, revelations.

Babaylan talaga—
  She nods in public
  because she doesn't get what people are saying in English.

She nods in public
  because she doesn't really care.

2. Lolo / grandpa:
He brews teas, herbs, draws his dreams to us.
asks his children and grandchildren to follow
their dreams.

Asks us to dance our fantasies on a linoleum floor,
and in a basement shag carpet in the northside of Chicago.

Sings:
> *tiro tiro bacaldo bonsay narang tamoro...*
>> calls on the sharks circles of his ocean.

Sings:
> make this recipe & nightmares won't be so heavy on your head.

Says:
> crush the luya for salabat (rhizome pungence to ward off worries).
> drop a fork (a visitor who is two-faced is on the way).
> Sing low & slow over your soup (it's just fun to do)!

Says to us:
> Where did your dream go, apo?
>> *tiro tiro bacaldo.*

> Where did your dream go

>>>> apo?

3. Mama:
Nightmare after nightmare.
An oracle professed:
  (Don't go under water)
  (Don'tgounderwater)
  <u>Dontgounderwater</u>

I was born wishing for scales.
  in tagalog
    in pangasinan
      in english

I wished for scales
and they never came
      she testified.

Due to an aversion to water, she played hard to get
by Lake Michigan. To be an ocean child and have disputes with shells!
Thumb prints engraved on rosary beads every time she saw a boat.
Fact is, she married a sailor with stars tattooed on his forearms
for insurance. I am sure there are more reasons, but context is
  important.

Mama mentioned to her 11 year old,
  I   *will*   *die*   *under*   *water.*

And she did
die

Lungs
barely
bouyed
in
fluid

her breath like
fluttered
       fins
until
       the
very
       end.

mixed race in mackinaw city #2

by age 7, he knew he was a chemistry set of blood samples:
pilipin@ blood for summer sweat, outdoor smoke from the grill,
arm and fist flung for protest or fishing boats beachside. his
body bridge for ocean wave snap unlikely pared with rural lake
michigan blizzard watches, canned jams stocked in shelves too
tall for the arms of children to reach without stool or a macgyver
improv of folgers rusted coffee cans.

he saw how his white washed and country town pulled their
lighter whiter skinned children closer when he and his mom
finished with church. how they were the brownest people there,
their knee joints bent pew after pew, station after station, his
mother's open handed "glory bes" struck discord with the clasped
close hands of their more fairer reserved jesus. that jesus didn't
take kindly to pork bbq on altars over suka dishes lace with sili.
mackinaw city 1988: the plastic decals like melted marshmellows
bubbled over the windows. they were meant to be snowflakes. this
is pre-hipster decals of birds and spirals and floral design, mind
you. my mama wanted the amerikan dream so badly, she stuck fake
snow stickers over wide trailer park windows overlooking what?
a snowstorm. a good two-footer to be precise. all great for snow
mobile leaps and sledding steep hills. she made fruitcake with
gelatinous sparkly cherries. she had hot cocoa as default beverage.
we all wore cosby sweaters pre-pudding pop commercials and
wore them after deer season, the venison chucked on 4x4s for
winter meat.

she either embraced or harshly wore this curse of negative wind
chill. it was hard to tell some days which it was and oddly, could
of been a mixture of the two. either way, she took on middle
americana and her face looking for a prize won after a long-hard
fight. Problem was, the fight was still happening. on snow days,

we would read from books at the table, the green dinette of metal legs received soft kicks from my tiny feet pronouncing vowel sounds, bigger words, words that he was told could get him outta this small town.

overheard were tagalog records and cassette tapes, mama singing to herself. humming *love songs to people i may never meet*, he thought as a teenager. thinking back on that moment, she was the only person in the whole city who actually knew the lyrics, knew them and could comprehend them, believe them. she was the only person who knew the song even existed. his scrawny face had big pink glasses parked on an even scrawnier nose bridge. he would ask between giraffe-sized english phonetics, "what does mahal mean, mama?" i chirped. "it means love, anak. say it with me," and she would take the hand of a spoon and stir her arroz caldo or her caldereta, teaching him the first call and response as snowflakes made glitter skids over their doorways. an act of resistance between the two of them set in a trailer home, winter whirling wind like laying down basic beats.

this is before they stormed out during the racist comments after a play in chicago, before she mournfully disagreed yet understood why their face was on TFC Fil-Am news talking about wars and anti-military. after all, he was putting those big words they'd accumulated through time to what they thought was good use. at the very beginning, it was the two of them mouthing consonants, she remembering and him learning anew, their cheeks reddened by frost that fought with their veins. not far in the distance, above the busy stove top, the browned kitchen window rattled to icicles, it's curtains covering rusted screws bunting out of alabaster caulk.

tools to survive mercury in retrograde

hide. don't read old journals, you'll hate your poetry because let's face it, no. burrow your head into every crease of the bed. talk to no one. embrace the mercurial... by yourself. take everything personally. take heed of your sharpness. take stock of your softness. watch youtube vids of fluffy pudgy baby animals. keep protein close. let the aches in, they're choreographed to the impending storm clouds anyway. reach out once then curl into your skin to the speed of raindrops. take nothing personally. light candles. crave any random set of foods not at your disposal. much better to crave green mango shakes & pompano rather than the people they remind you of. regret doesn't deserve an answer. believe it or not, now is not the time for 90's r&b jams, salty snacks, the gluttonous. make sure no one quotes you on that last statement. hollow to the radius of any loss or any win. let the wind through this gap of you. remember, the guilt wasn't yours to keep. wipe residue off your altar. let the rain on your face be a proper disguise. drink cups of water on the hour. let the dogs be a shield of oxytocins & paw pads. if you can't howl, pay no mind, your joints will do it for you. you know this already. clasp knees to your chest. lullaby it out. love. let her go. want. let them go. don't eat all the pastries in the fridge. the problem isn't that you are not enough, the gift is that you are incredibly all too much. hum yourself through, your spirit will do it for you. if crumpled up, now is not the time to underestimate yourself: the fetal position is a damn fine place to write.

Sumput Kalad Abong

On this day two years ago I massaged her legs,
arms, watched them buoy in mid-air like balloons, like containers
filled to the brim. was this yesterday? I don't agree with the flower
industry, roses and tulips being grown in homelands like mine,
chemicals caught in eyelashes and in people's throats. The
workers not being compensated for their labor. Insecticides,
herbicides, fungicides, and soil fumigants, all pollutants into
the skin for thousands of workers. But this is what my mom
wanted, roses like every mother celebrating mother's day.
I spent the little money I had and gave her the roses.

I had the inability to become a safe doctor or lawyer, a
financially responsible engineer, even a drab heterosexual
person. I couldn't stay in doors for protests and couldn't hold
my tongue back. I actually told her I stopped eating pork
altogether. The least I could do was buy flowers, follow the
usual mother's day protocol.

She coughed up blood, liquid swelling in her lungs, a cough
she said, a cold she said. I wonder why the doctor
lied to her and signed that medical permission slip so that
she could travel across the ocean 23 hours later, back to
her home. He must've known. He must've known she was
practically gone. His pen swirled slopes like the airplanes
they've both traveled, he smiled softly and probably kept it
quiet or unsaid. Maybe the both of them realized the truce—
he her doctor and she her patient, or perhaps something more
human like migrant to migrant. the cancer had spread and her
heart, lungs, kidney, they all were slowly deteriorating.
she had to go home.

All I could do was try to massage it out of her. I received hilot
every instance I had a trace of a sore throat, achy muscle, sad
heart as a child. Old and young women came to my house
after the women healers in my family had died and pressed
my body into circular patterns, their fingers stirring camphor
in the air, their faces controlled and confident. I am no healer
like this. I could only do what I could to appease the body
from spilling from itself. the mountainous mattress springs
of her small studio basement apartment creaked from the weight.

I could only cry and tell her to come back to me. Put the
socks on her feet one by one, help her with her sweater,
then her coat, carry her purse, make sure her passport
was in order. My palm felt as minute as it was at age 8 after the
first heart attack, brushing it across her forehead and with the
same childhood hope, thinking that was just enough.

And I sang to her, in a low and trembling voice,

gala sumpit kalad abong, agka na tatakot.
(Come on, let's go home, there's no need to be afraid)

My lola sang this to me as I dangled from her sturdy body as
thick as an aged tree, both our eyes half-asleep in crescent
moons, drifting in Chicago starlight. My titas sang this when
the small babies unfurled cries from the cars to the front steps.
As is the only way to keep new spirits safe. All of us, the cousins,
aunts and my ma would be a choir on the sidewalk
leading to the stoop steps.

When fear is this close, when you can see the body has taken
on too much even for its own architecture, it may seem
beyond repairable, hopeless. What is there to do but sing the
helplessness into a rhythm that can sustain us, even for the
last seconds?

I pulled her up from her bed, handed her her cane. Her eyes
were like caves, I remember. I told her to eat all of her favorite
foods, santol, oyster from the shell, smell the beach please,
tell her I will be there soon. Bring me sand... and snacks.
Say to say hi to lolo and lola for me in their graves. She nodded.

I asked her to stretch everyday, rotate her wrists, her neck,
ask my cousins to massage her back and legs since I couldn't
be there. I pressed my lips at her forehead, helped her into
the car. She clutched my fingers, and like every mountain
holding the pour of the rain, she got soft, her face buried something.

The men in her apartment were kind enough to drive
her to the airport, usher her to inside. Their workdays of metal,
grease, and dirt under their nails, they'd hold her up passed the
doorway. One panicked, let his stern composure crack,
manang, maybe you should cancel? Kasi, the hospitals are
better here. Her face looking forward, her throat filled with liquid.
No, let's go. It's time.

I asked her to promise to come back to me, safe and whole.
She promised those fake treaties just to appease, just to make
amends, just in case. If she couldn't promise her return she
knew I would never let her get near an airport gate, she knew
I could talk her into anything, it was my gift after all. I couldn't
pay rent with it, but I could argue her to stay in another hospital
bed somewhere in Humboldt park without ever going back
home. Besides, isn't the responsibility of a mother to ensure
security, to believe that even the impossible can occur? She got
here to this country in spite of oceans and odds, she had a child,
she did what she came to do, hadn't she? Kahit anong yahiri,
Anything is possible, anak ko.

Two years ago I cried all day. Called my lover, and I tried
to voice it by phone wires, tried to explain that I knew she's

never going to come back. Another promise you grow up with, prepped & knew that when the time came, if you were both lucky, you would be given this moment. An immigrant's child sensibilities
are smart and they know how to scar.

I walked on kedzie ave., watched for the car to turn around carefully walked blocks like needle to thread, hoping she'd find her way back to my hands.

Acknowledgements and Gratitude

Thank you to my political, poetry, art, support, and community pamilya namely: Geleni Fontaine, Aemilius Ramirez, Mel G. Campbell, Kiyaan Abadani, Kit Yan, Ryka Aoki, Oliver Bendorf, Nico Amador, Cris Izaguirre, Sarwat Rumi, Elakshi Kumar, Ejeris Dixon, Ryan Li Dahlstrom, Setareh Mohammadi, Manish Vaidya, Sonia Guiñansaca, Sham-e-ali Nayeem, Ola Osaze, Bekah Fly, Bamby Salcedo, emi koyama, Shonnetia Monique, Amir Rabiyyah, Victor Tobar, Bao Phi, Leah Lakshmi Piepzna-Samarasinha, Fabian Romero, Ann Russo, Francesca Royster, Akemi Nishida, Karen Hanna, Rhoda Rae Gutierrez, Stacey Milbern, Laila Farah, Lani Montreal, Arti Mehta, Prerna Sampat, Brianne Moore, Dean Jackson, Ro Garrido, Idalia R De León, Ki'tay Davidson, Mia Nakano, Mitali Punchali, Gerónimo Lempira, Ezak Perez, William Maria Rain, Rebecca Connie, Quinton Guyton, Richard Nioti Vanderpuije, Sharmili Majmudar, Amita Swadhin, Mikal Hemingway, Ignacio Rivera, Brandon Lacey-Campos, Taueret Davis, Leroy Moore, Cherry Gallette, Julz Ignacio, Jai Dulani, Tahira Pratt, Patty Berne, Morgan H. Goode, Natalia Lopez, Sofia Webster, Erin O'Brien, Fayise Mohamed Ahmed Abrahim, Celiany Velásquez Rivera, Ang Garcia, Beatriz Beckford, Lucia Leandro Gimeno, Suze Lusive, Ignacio Rivera, Jay Toole, Alexis Pauline

Gumbs, Almah LaVon Rice-Faina, Sarah Joseph Kurien, Avinash Rajagopal, Fatima Arain, Lauren Francisco, Piali Muhkerjee, Nik Lal, Kiwi Illafonte, Eli Claire, R. Erica Doyle, Sebastian Margaret, Anida Ali, Yalini Dream, D'Lo, Ashley Young, Tara Betts, Nikki Patin, Sharon Bridgforth, Adelina Anthony, Anna Saini, Denise Ruiz, Olivia Trinidad Canlas, Jill Aguado, Edith Bucio, Ashley Young, Phoebe Connoly Pam Nuchols, Red Durkin, Kelli Dunham, Fresh White, Jim Andralis, Darlene Torres.

Some of these poems were written for & because of: Mango Tribe, Gabriela Network, Mangoes With Chili, Dark Sciences: A QPOC Dream Retreat 2015, Teatro QPOC Residency 2013, The Disability Justice Collective, Sins Invalid, Sick & Disabled Queers FB Group.

This book spans the U.S. Empire all the way to the Pilipinas, through the wires of LiveJournal, and into my dreams.

PHOTO: *Karen Campos Castillo*

About The Author

KAY ULANDAY BARRETT aka brownroundboi, is a poet, performer, and educator, navigating life as a disabled pilipinx-amerikan transgender queer in the U.S. with struggle, resistance, and laughter. K. has featured on colleges & stages globally; Princeton University, UC Berkeley, Musee Pour Rire in Montreal, and The Chicago Historical Society. K's bold work continues to excite and challenge audiences. K. has facilitated workshops, presented keynotes, and contributed to panels with various social justice communities. Honors include: Chicago's LGBTQ 30 under 30 awards, Finalist for The Gwendolyn Brooks Open-Mic Award, Windy City Times Pride Literary Poetry Prize. He is a recent Poetry Fellow at The Home School whose contributions are found in PBS News Hour Poetry, Poor Magazine, Trans Bodies/Trans Selves, Windy City Queer: Dispatches from the Third Coast, Make/Shift, Third Woman Press, The Advocate, and Bitch Magazine. K. turns art into action and is dedicated to remixing recipes. Recent publications include contributions in the upcoming anthologies, "Outside the XY: Queer Black & Brown Masculinity" and "Writing the Walls Down: A Convergence of LGBTQ Voices." See their work at KAYBARRETT.NET.

About Heliotrope

Heliotrope is a dedicated series of poetry books by transgender authors. We value writing which is sincere, direct, self-aware, formally resourceful, and which tells a story (or several). The poetry we publish is a challenge. It's a tool, but it's also a dare to use that tool: to talk more; to think harder; to believe in yourself *and* question yourself; maybe even to write some poems of your own.

In 2016, Heliotrope will publish books by KOKUMO, Cat Fitzpatrick, and Kay Ulanday Barrett.

Heliotrope is an imprint of Topside Press and is edited by Cat Fitzpatrick. Cat teaches literature at Rutgers University - Newark and organizes the Trans Poets Workshop NYC.

Poets are welcome to join the Trans Poets Workshop- more information at transpoets.com

Submissions of poetry manuscripts are welcome year-round at topsidepress.com